Science That's Appropriate <u>and</u> Doable

This science resource book was written with two goals in mind:

- to provide "good" science for your students
- to make it easy for you

What makes this book "good" science?

When you follow the step-by-step lessons in this book, you'll be using an instructional model that makes science education relevant to real life.

- Your students will be drawn in by interesting activities that encourage them to express what they already know about a concept.

- Your students will participate in hands-on discovery experiences and be guided to describe the experiences in their own words. Together, you'll record the experiences in both class and individual logbooks.

- You'll provide explanations and vocabulary that will help your students accurately explain what they have experienced.

- Your students will have opportunities to apply their new understandings to new situations.

What makes this book easy for you?

- The step-by-step activities are easy to understand and have illustrations where it's important.

- The resources you need are at your fingertips — record sheets; logbook forms; and other reproducibles such as minibooks, task cards, picture cards, and pages to make into overhead transparencies.

- Each science concept is presented in a self-contained section. You can decide to do the entire book or pick only those sections that enhance your own curriculum.

For sites on the World Wide Web that supplement the material in this resource book, go to http://www.evan-moor.com and look for the Product Updates link on the main page.

Using Logbooks as Learning Tools

Logbooks are valuable learning tools for several reasons:
- Logbooks give students an opportunity to put what they are learning into their own words.
- Putting ideas into words is an important step in internalizing new information. Whether spoken or written, this experience allows students to synthesize their thinking.
- Explaining and describing experiences help students make connections between several concepts and ideas.
- Logbook entries allow the teacher to catch misunderstandings right away and then reteach.
- Logbooks are a useful reference for students and a record of what has been learned.

Two Types of Logbooks

The Class Logbook

A class logbook is completed by the teacher and the class together. The teacher records student experiences and helps students make sense of their observations. The class logbook is a working document. You will return to it often for a review of what has been learned. As new information is acquired, make additions and corrections to the logbook.

Individual Science Logbooks

Individual students process their own understanding of investigations by writing their own responses in their own logbooks. Two types of logbook pages are provided in this unit.

1. Open-ended logbook pages:
   Pages 4 and 5 provide two choices of pages that can be used to respond to activities in the unit. At times you may wish students to write in their own logbooks and then share their ideas as the class logbook entry is made. After the class logbook has been completed, allow students to revise and add information to their own logbooks. At other times you may wish students to copy the class logbook entry into their own logbooks.

2. Specific logbook pages:
   You will find record forms or activity sheets following many activities that can be added to each student's logbook.

At the conclusion of the unit, reproduce a copy of the logbook cover on page 3 for each student. Students can then organize both types of pages and staple them with the cover.

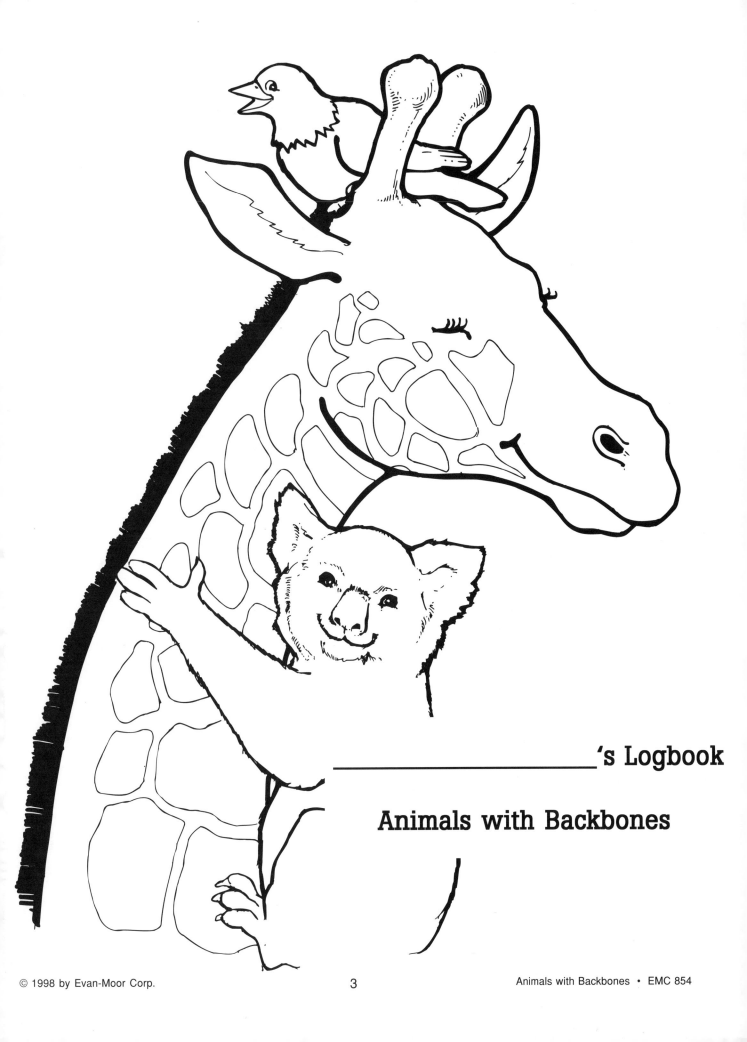

_____'s Logbook

Animals with Backbones

3

Name _____

This is what I learned about animals with backbones today:

Note: Reproduce this form for students to record science investigations for their individual logbooks.

Name ____________________________________

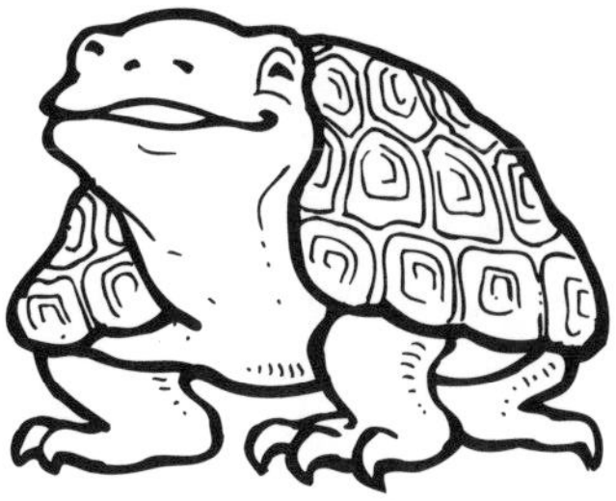

Investigation: ____________________________

What we did:

____

____

____

What we saw:

____

____

____

What we learned:

____

____

____

Animals with backbones are called vertebrates.

Some Animals Have a Backbone

- You will need the skeletons of a chicken and a fish. Clean all the meat off the bones, wash them thoroughly, and let dry. Place the skeletons on separate trays.

  Working with a small group at a time, have students examine the bones and name the ones they recognize. Point to the backbone of each animal. Ask, "Do you know what these skeleton bones are called? Is the skeleton inside or outside of the animal?" Provide the term "backbone" if students do not know the answer.

- Make overhead transparencies of the animal skeletons on pages 8 and 9. Show the transparencies and call on students to point out the backbone on each.

- Reproduce page 10 for each student. Have them locate and circle each animal's backbone.

- Begin a class logbook with a page entitled "Backbones." Have students copy the logbook entry for their individual logbooks using the form on page 4.

Backbones

Some kinds of animals have a backbone.

These animals have a skeleton inside.

Check with a high school science department to see if they have skeletons you can borrow. Borrow x-rays of animals from a veterinarian. Take a field trip to a natural history museum to see skeletons.

Backbone/No Backbone

- Discuss how to tell if an animal has a backbone by looking at the animal. (If you touched it and felt bones under the skin, it probably has a backbone. If it looks like an animal you know has a backbone, it probably has a backbone. If it looks soft and squishy, it probably doesn't have a backbone. If it has an outside shell or skeleton, it doesn't have a backbone.)

- Reproduce the picture cards on pages 11–14. Pass out the cards, one per person. Have students decide if their card shows an animal with a backbone or an animal without a backbone. Have them explain their decisions.

If you feel your students are ready, introduce the term "vertebrates" at this time.

Animal Search

- Give each student a clipboard (see sample below) and go for an "animal walk" around the neighborhood to find examples of animals with backbones. Have students record the animals they see.

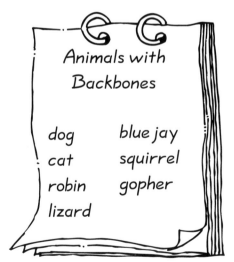

- Back in class, list the animals they observed on the chalkboard. Point to each animal on the list and ask, "Does the animal have a backbone?" Erase any invertebrates from the list. Record the names of the animals remaining on a class logbook page entitled "Animals with Backbones."

frog skeleton

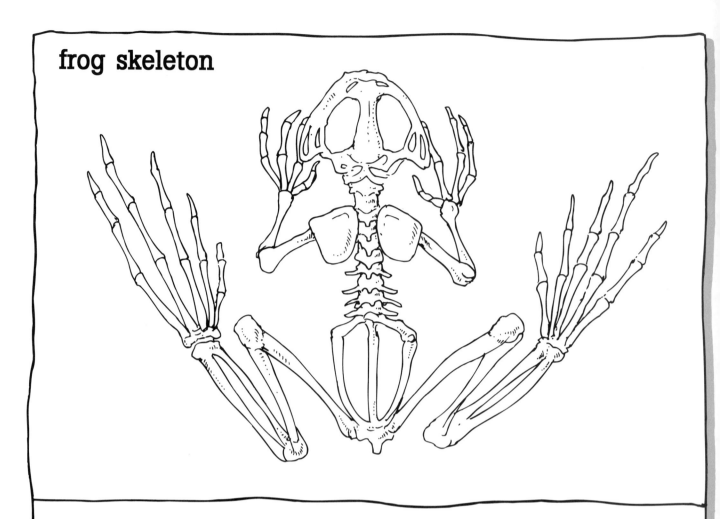

fish skeleton

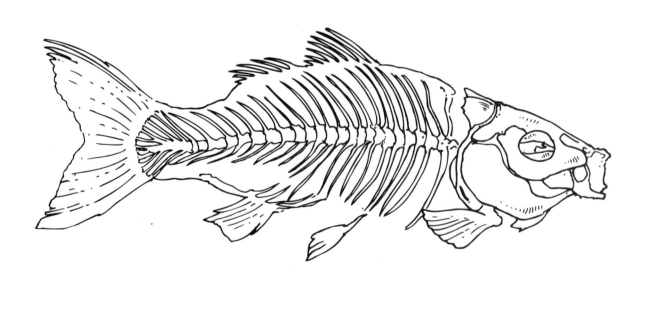

8

lizard skeleton

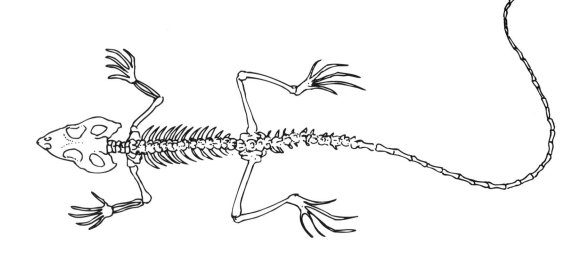

cat skeleton

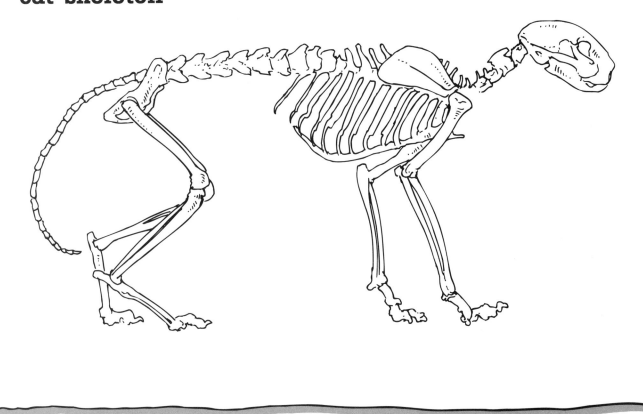

Animals with Backbones • EMC 854

Name _____

Find the Backbone

Circle the backbones.

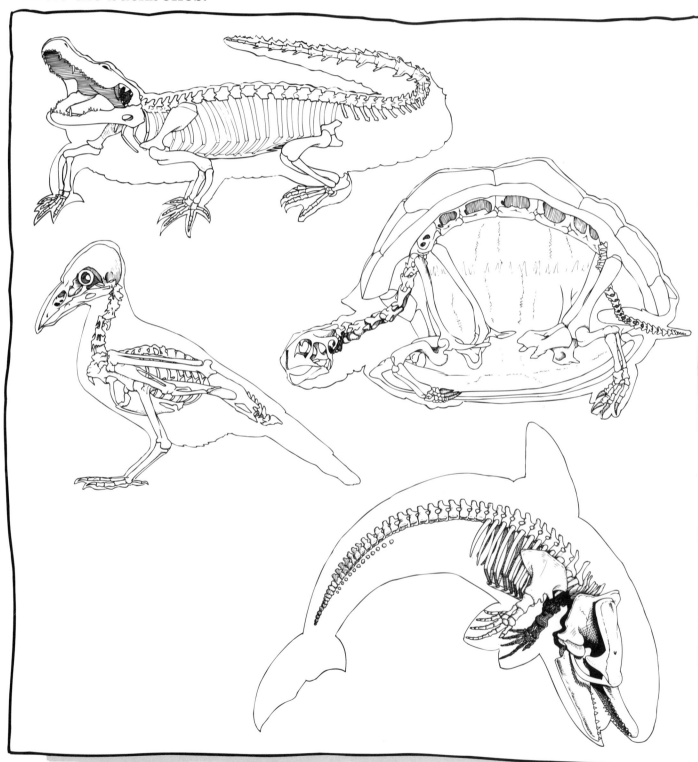

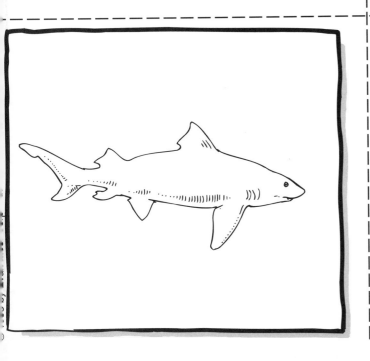

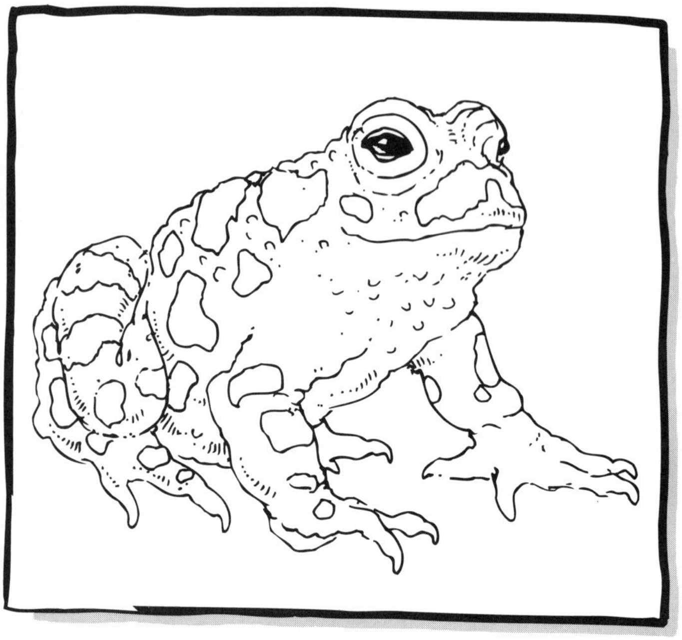

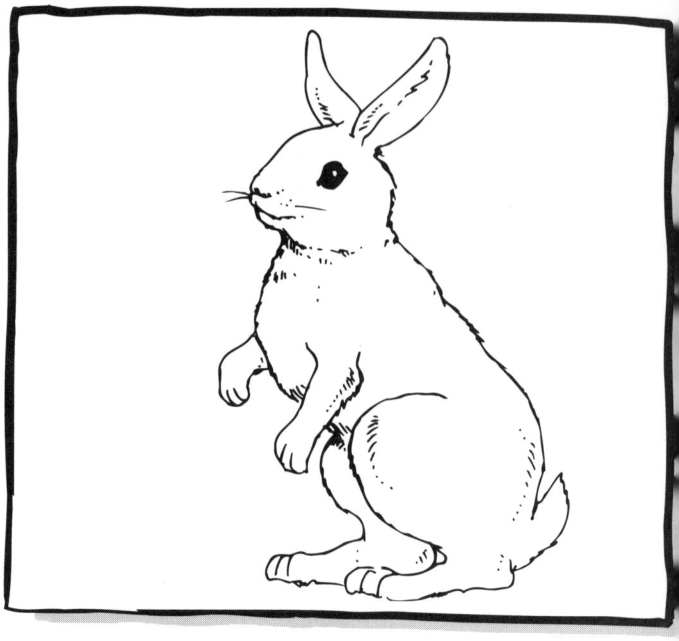

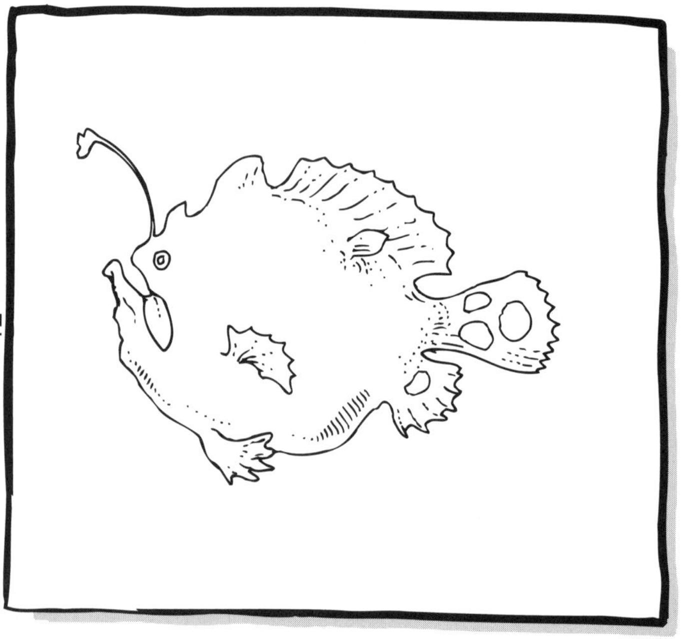

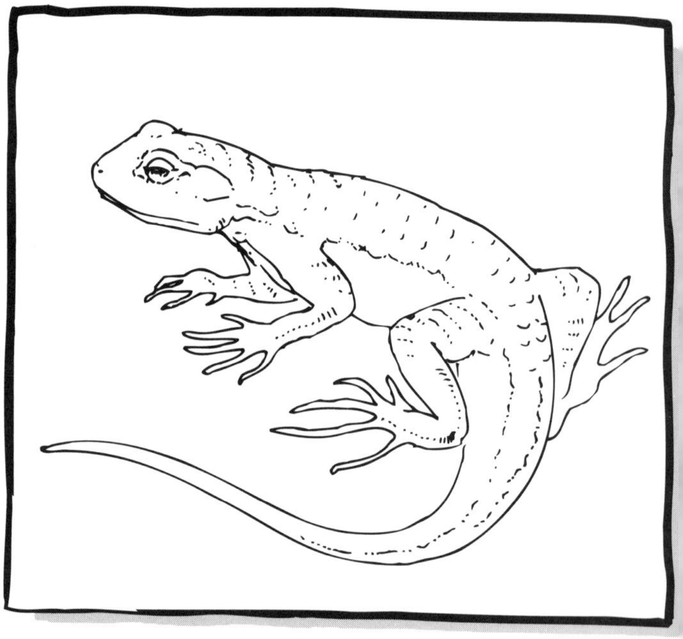

© 1998 by Evan-Moor Corp. Animals with Backbones • EMC 854

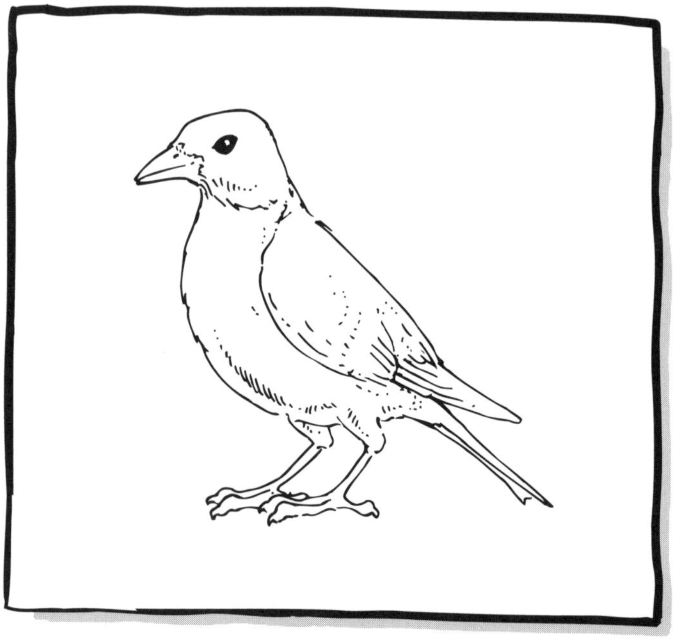

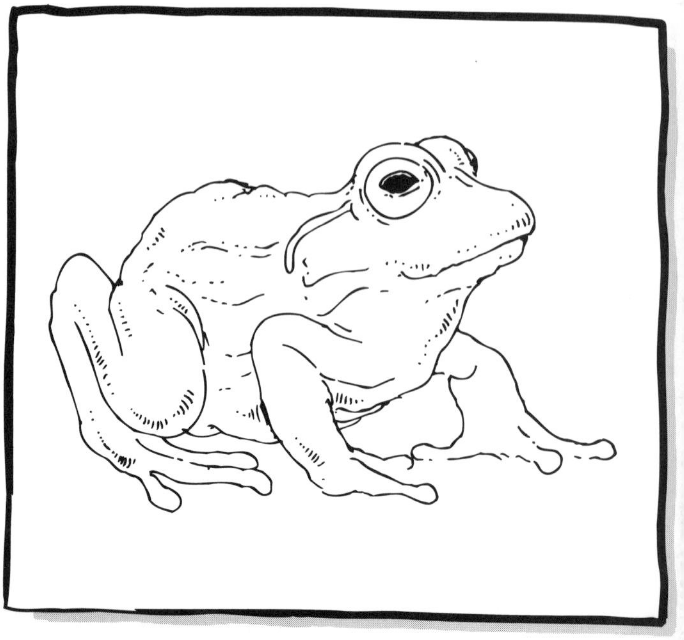

14

Vertebrates are classified by their body characteristics.

Preparation

Before beginning the rest of the unit on vertebrates, plan opportunities for students to observe animals.

- Plan field trips to places such as:

  a pet shop   a zoo
  an aquarium   an animal shelter
  neighborhood pet owners   a farm

- Invite people to bring animals to school:

  someone who collects birds, snakes, turtles, etc.
  a farmer with rabbits, chickens, a baby goat, etc.
  an animal shelter staff member with a wild vertebrate

- Keep animals in class:

  a terrarium with a turtle or lizard
  an aquarium with a frog or toad
  an aquarium with several kinds of fish
  a cage with a small bird
  a cage with a hamster, gerbil, rabbit, or mouse

Be sure to research proper care before bringing an animal into the classroom.

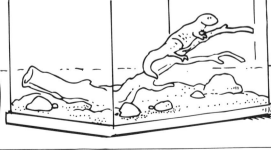

Five Groups of Vertebrates

- Divide a large sheet of paper into five groups. Explain to the class that they are going to learn about five groups of animals. Write the names in the boxes, one at a time, asking students to name animals that fit that group. Begin with birds and fish, as students will already recognize those group names. When you reach "reptile," say, "Can anyone name a reptile?" If no one can give a correct answer, say, "Garter snakes, box turtles, and crocodiles are reptiles. Can you think of any others?" List any of their suggestions. Continue with amphibians and mammals.

Brainstorm to list characteristics students think they know for each of the animal groups. Record all their ideas on the chart. Corrections will be made at a later time.

birds	fish	reptiles	amphibians	mammals
canary	goldfish	garter snake	frog	cat
parrot	catfish	crocodile	toad	dog
chicken	shark			bear
robin				

- Reproduce several sets of the cards on pages 11–14. Divide the class into small groups. Give a set of the vertebrate cards to each group. Have students sort the cards into the five vertebrate animal groups. Have the groups explain which cards they put together and why.

Observe and Record Physical Features

- Reproduce page 18 for students to use as they observe a live animal or view a video about an animal. They are to answer the questions and then draw the animal. (This form can be used again as students observe other animals.)

- Read books about each animal group. These books are a good starting place: *What Is a Fish?* by David Eastman (Troll Communications, 1982); *Reptiles and Amphibians* by Catherine Howell (National Geographic Society, 1994); *New True Books Bird Series* by Alice Flanagan (Children's Press, 1996); *Mammals* by Martyn Branwell (DK Publishing Inc., 1993). Ask students to recall what they learned from hearing the stories.

Vertebrate Minibooks

Each of the reproducible minibooks on pages 19–23 presents one of the five groups of vertebrates. Fold along the lines to form the book. Students will read each book to review the characteristics of that animal group.

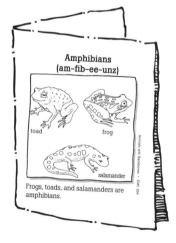

Characteristics of Vertebrates

Make a class logbook page for each vertebrate group, listing its characteristics. Reproduce five copies of page 4 for each student so they can copy the charts for their individual logbooks.

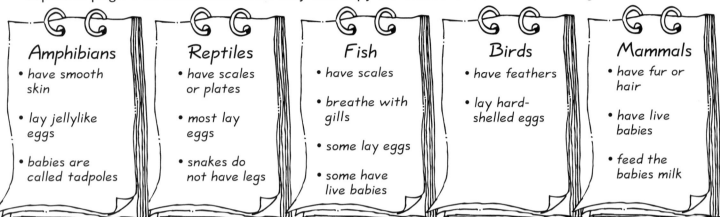

Amphibians
- have smooth skin
- lay jellylike eggs
- babies are called tadpoles

Reptiles
- have scales or plates
- most lay eggs
- snakes do not have legs

Fish
- have scales
- breathe with gills
- some lay eggs
- some have live babies

Birds
- have feathers
- lay hard-shelled eggs

Mammals
- have fur or hair
- have live babies
- feed the babies milk

Reporting on Vertebrates

Divide the class into five groups. Assign an animal group to each student group. Each member of the group paints an animal from their animal group. The whole group works together to make a chart, listing the characteristics of their animal group.

Display the completed work on a bulletin board entitled "Animals with Backbones" or "Vertebrates."

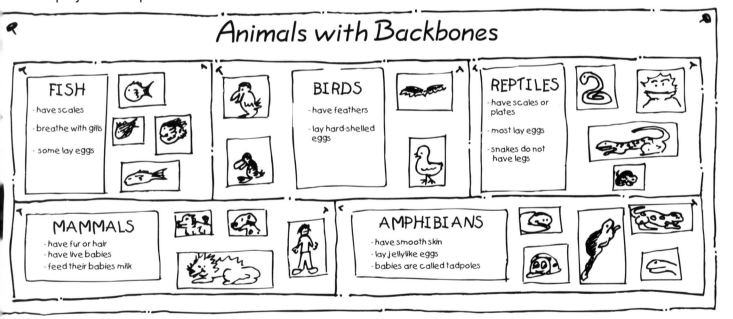

Check for Understanding

- Reproduce page 24 for each student. They are to read the description and then write the group to which the animals belong.

- Reproduce page 25 for each student. Have the students read a descriptive phrase and then mark all animal groups that share that characteristic.

Name _____

About _____
name of animal

Examine your animal.
Use a magnifying glass to see small parts.

1. How many legs do you see? _____

2. What kind of body cover does it have?

        scales   hair   skin

3. What color is it? _____

4. Does it have a tail? _____

5. Does it have gills or lungs? _____

Draw the animal.
Label its parts.

Animals with Backbones • EMC 854

Frogs, toads, and salamanders are amphibians.

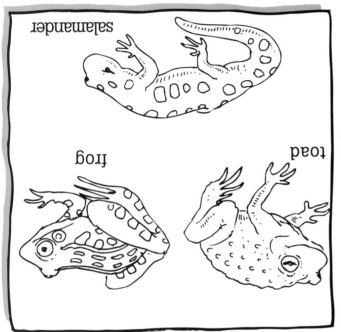

salamander

frog toad

Amphibians
(am-fib-ee-unz)

fold 1

fold 2

Some amphibians live on land when they grow up. Some stay in the water.

Most amphibians have smooth, moist skin.

They lay jellylike eggs in water. The babies live in the water.

1

Tuna, sharks, and seahorses are fish.

shark

seahorse

tuna

Fish

fold 1

fold 2

4

Most kinds of fish lay eggs. Some kinds have live babies.

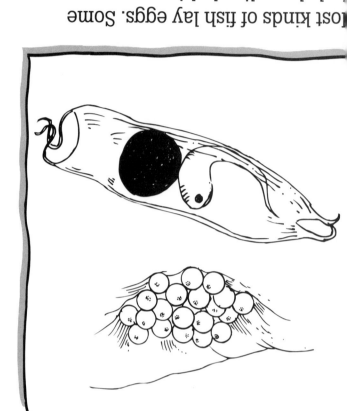

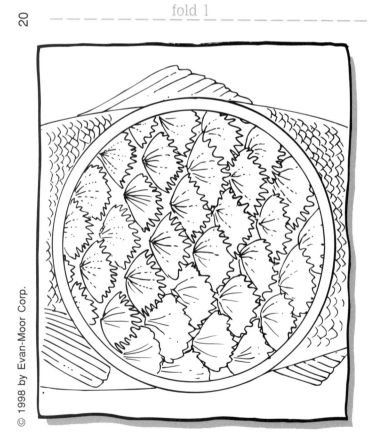

Fish have scales.

2

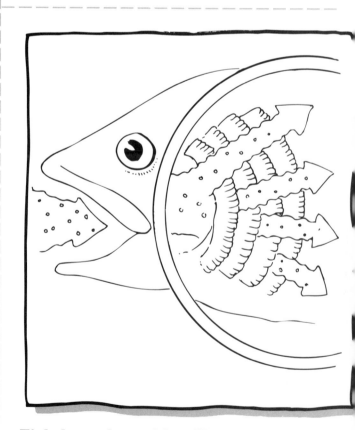

Fish breathe with gills.

3

Turtles, snakes, and alligators are reptiles.

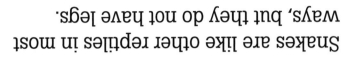

snake

turtle

alligator

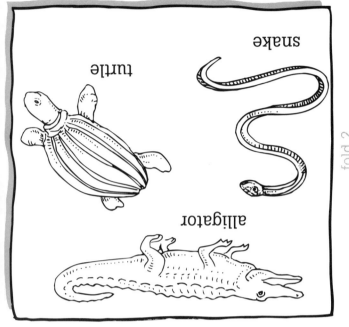

Reptiles
(rep-tilz)

fold 1

Snakes are like other reptiles in most ways, but they do not have legs.

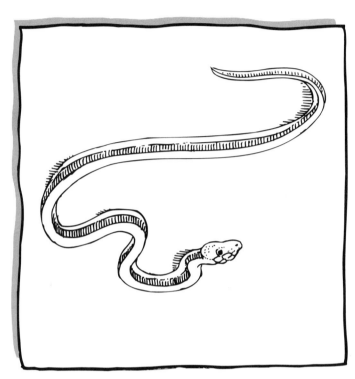

fold 2

Reptiles are covered with scales or plates.

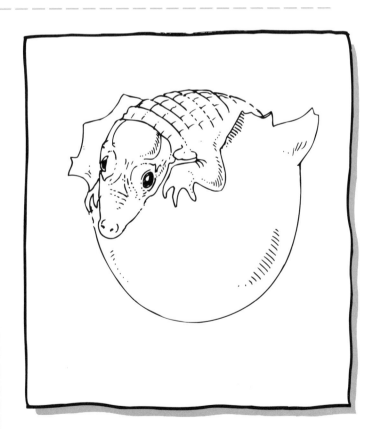

Most reptiles lay eggs.

Rabbits, monkeys, and dogs are mammals.

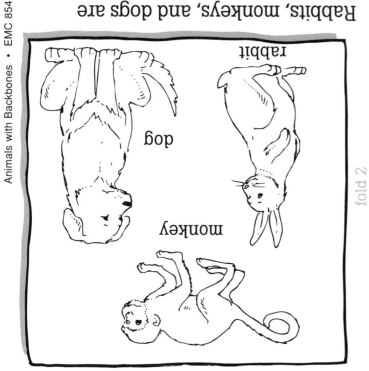

dog

rabbit

monkey

Mammals (mam-ulz)

Animals with Backbones • EMC 854

fold 1

fold 2

...platypus and a spiny anteater are ...ammals, but they lay eggs.

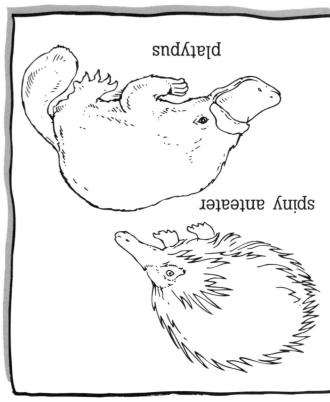

platypus

spiny anteater

polar bear

African elephant

Mammals have hair or fur. Some have a little. Some have a lot.

2

Almost all mammal babies are born alive. The babies are fed milk from their mothers.   3

Birds

Chickens, robins, and owls are birds.

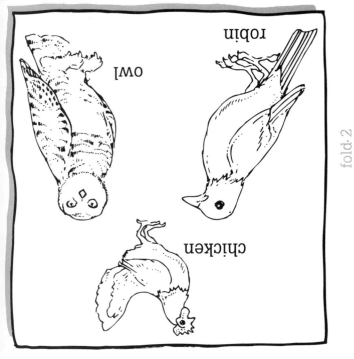

owl
robin
chicken

1

Most birds can fly.
A penguin is a bird that cannot fly.

4

All birds have feathers.

2

Baby birds hatch from eggs. Bird eggs have hard shells.

3

fold 1

fold 2

Name _____

What Am I?

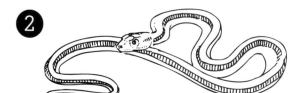

Write the animal group under each picture.

fish   birds   amphibians   reptiles   mammals

Robins have feathers.
The female lays hard-shelled eggs.

Robins are_____.

Garter snakes have scales.
The female lays rubbery eggs.

Garter snakes are_____.

Frogs have smooth, damp skin.
The female lays jellylike eggs.

Frogs are_____.

Rabbits have hair.
The female feeds her babies milk.

Rabbits are_____.

Tuna have scales.
Tuna breathe with gills.

Tuna are _____.

Turtles have scales.
Turtles breathe with lungs.

Turtles are_____.

24

Animals with Backbones • EMC 854

Name _____

Is It True?

Check the box if the statement is true about most animals in the group.

	amphibians	reptiles	fish	birds	mammals
1. have a backbone					
2. have scales					
3. have smooth skin					
4. breathe with gills					
5. breathe with lungs					
6. have fur or hair					
7. have feathers					
8. have feet with claws or fingernails					
9. lay eggs with hard shells					
10. feed milk to babies					

Vertebrates change as they grow.

Puppy to Dog—A Mammal Life Cycle

- Read *My Puppy Is Born* by Joanna Cole (Morrow Junior, 1991) or *Our Puppies Are Growing* by Carolyn Otto (Harper Collins, 1998). Discuss how the puppies changed as they grew. Allow time for students to share their own experiences with raising pets.

- Invite a small puppy and its owner to visit class several times over a period of weeks or months so students can observe the changes that happen. Reproduce multiple copies of the observation form on page 30 for each student. Staple the copies together to make an observation booklet for each student. Weigh and measure the puppy on each visit. Have students record these figures and draw the puppy each visit.

- Write a page entitled "Dog Life Cycle" for the class logbook.

- Read *Animals Born Alive and Well* by Ruth Heller (Grosset & Dunlap, 1982). Discuss the characteristics common to all mammal young *(babies born alive; fed with mother's milk)*. Ask students to recall how the spiny anteater and duckbill platypus differ from other mammals *(lay eggs)*.

Dog Life Cycle

Puppies are born alive.

The mother feeds them milk.

They grow bigger every day.

When the puppies are grown, they can have babies, too.

Tadpole to Frog—An Amphibian Life Cycle

- Collect frog eggs from a pond or stream (look for pictures of frog eggs to serve as an identification guide) or order them from a science supply catalog. Raise the eggs in class so students can observe the stages a tadpole passes through as it changes into a frog.

- Post an observation chart next to the frog egg container. Once a week have a student observer write the date and record any changes that have occurred.

Materials

- aquarium or large jar
- pond or stream water, mud, and small plants
- algae-covered rocks
- frog eggs (or tadpoles if no eggs are available)

Steps to Follow

1. Place rocks, mud, and plants in the aquarium or jar.
2. Add the pond water and frog eggs (or tadpoles).
3. **Do not change the water!** The young tadpoles will eat the algae and small green plants. Older ones can be fed ground beef and chopped worms. (Only use a small amount at a time. Uneaten food will spoil.)
4. Watch as they grow and change. When they get four legs, cover the container with a screen. Make sure there is an area where the young frogs can get out of the water. Return the full-grown frogs to the pond.

Follow Up

- Write a page entitled "Frog Life Cycle" for the class logbook, listing the changes students have observed.

- Reproduce the logbook form on page 5 for each student and have them complete it for their individual logbooks. (Students may need help recalling what they did to set up the aquarium as they fill in "What we did.")

- Read *From Tadpole to Frog* by Wendy Pfeffer (Harper Collins, 1994), or watch a video on the life cycle of a frog. Ask students to recall what changes happened as the tadpoles grew. List these on the chalkboard. Compare the changes to those recorded on the class observation chart. Make additions or corrections to the "Frog Life Cycle" logbook page. (You may want to introduce the term "metamorphosis" at this time.)

Chick to Hen — A Bird Life Cycle

• Read *See How They Grow* by Jane Burton (Lodestar Books, 1992). Ask students to recall what happens to the egg, then to the chick, as it grows.

• If you have access to an outdoor area where you can put a pen, have your class hatch eggs in an incubator and raise chickens. (It is important to find a final home for the chicks **before** starting this activity.)

If raising chicks seems overwhelming, find a local poultry person who is willing to bring chicks to class once every two weeks so students can observe the changes that occur. Weigh and measure the chicks. Reproduce multiple copies of the observation form on page 30 for each student to make an observation booklet. Students record the measurements and draw the chicken at each observation.

• Show a video or filmstrip on the life cycle of a chicken. Then write a page entitled "A Bird Life Cycle" for the class logbook.

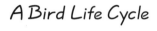

A Bird Life Cycle

Birds hatch from eggs.

They are little and wet.

They get fluffy when they dry.

The birds grow bigger every day.

When birds are grown, they have babies, too.

Animals with Backbones • EMC 854

- Read *Chickens Aren't the Only Ones* by Ruth Heller (Grosset & Dunlap, 1981). Recall all the vertebrates that lay eggs. List these on the chalkboard. Use this information to create a class book entitled "What Is in This Egg?"

Materials

- pages 31 and 32, reproduced on construction paper for each student
- scissors
- glue
- crayons

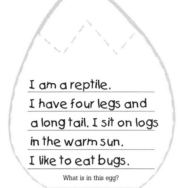

I am a reptile.
I have four legs and a long tail. I sit on logs in the warm sun.
I like to eat bugs.

What is in this egg?

Steps to Follow

1. Cut out the large egg. Draw an animal that hatches from an egg on the bottom half of the page. Write the animal's name below the picture.
2. Cut out the cracked egg shell. Write a riddle about the animal on the shell. Put glue on the marked section. Place it over the drawing.
3. Place all of the eggs together in a construction paper cover. Staple at the top to make a class book.

Fish and Reptile Life Cycles

Most young reptiles and fish hatch from eggs. Share examples of these life cycles in the following ways:

- Read books such as *A Fish Hatches* by Joanna Cole (Morrow Junior, 1978) and show videos or filmstrips of the life cycles of reptiles and fish. Ask students to recall how the animals change as they grow. Record the information on pages for the class logbook.

- Reproduce page 33 (Life Cycle of a Fish) and page 34 (Life Cycle of a Reptile) for each student. They are to cut out the pictures and paste them in the correct order to illustrate the life cycle.

"Animals Change and Grow" Minibook

- Reproduce pages 35–39 for each student to use when reviewing vertebrate life cycles. Compare the ways the cycles are the same and discuss how they are different.

- Have students use all the information they have learned about vertebrate life cycles to write a definition of "Life Cycle" for the class logbook. Reproduce copies of the logbook form on page 4 for each student. Have them copy the definition for their individual logbooks.

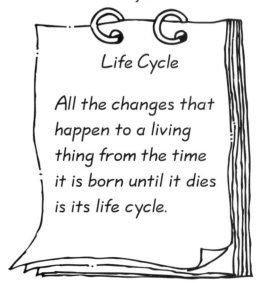

Life Cycle

All the changes that happen to a living thing from the time it is born until it dies is its life cycle.

Note: Reproduce this form multiple times to make the observation booklet described on pages 26 and 28.

My____________________ Record Book

type of animal

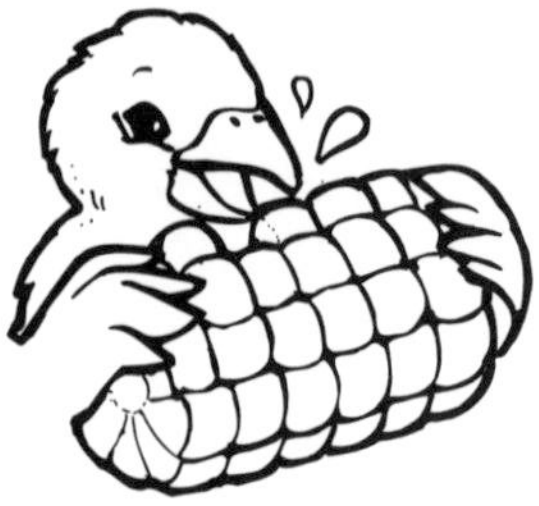

Name ____________________

Date ____________________

Draw the animal.

It weighs this much: ____________________

It is this long: ____________________

I saw these changes: ____________________

____

____

Note: Reproduce the patterns on this and the following page for students to use with page 29.

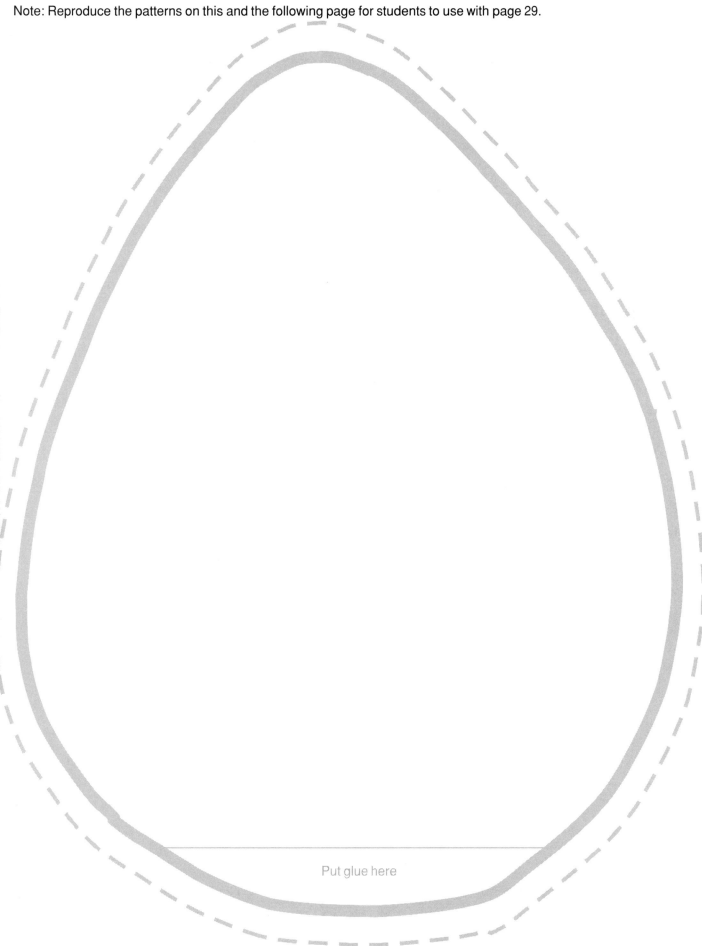

Put glue here

Animals with Backbones • EMC 854

_____

_____

_____

_____

_____

What is in this egg?

put glue on back

Animals with Backbones • EMC 854

Name _____

Cut out the pictures.
Paste them in order.

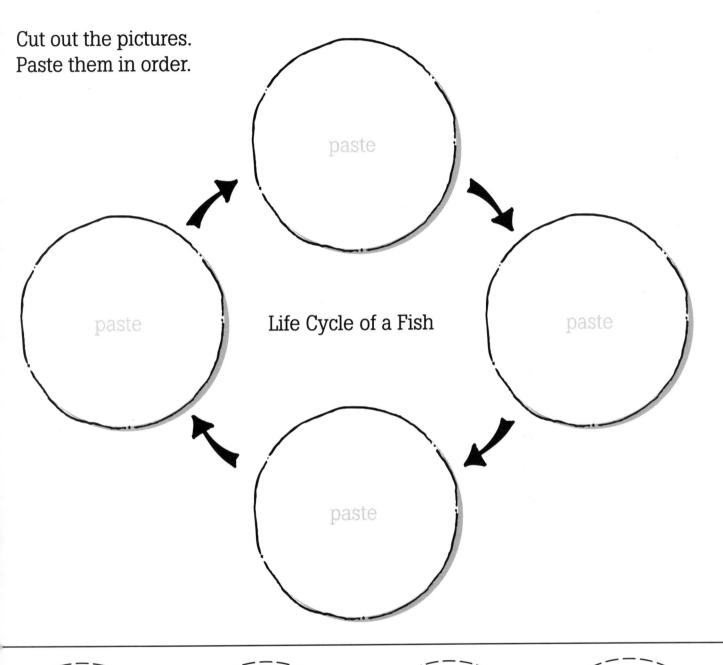

Life Cycle of a Fish

paste

paste

paste

paste

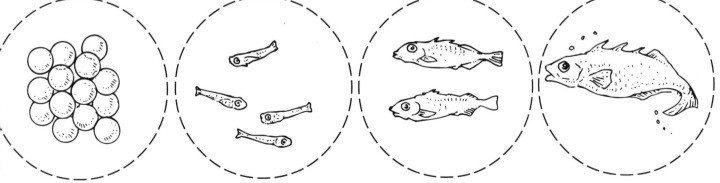

Note: Reproduce this sequencing activity for each student to use with page 29.

Name ____

Cut out the pictures.
Paste them in order.

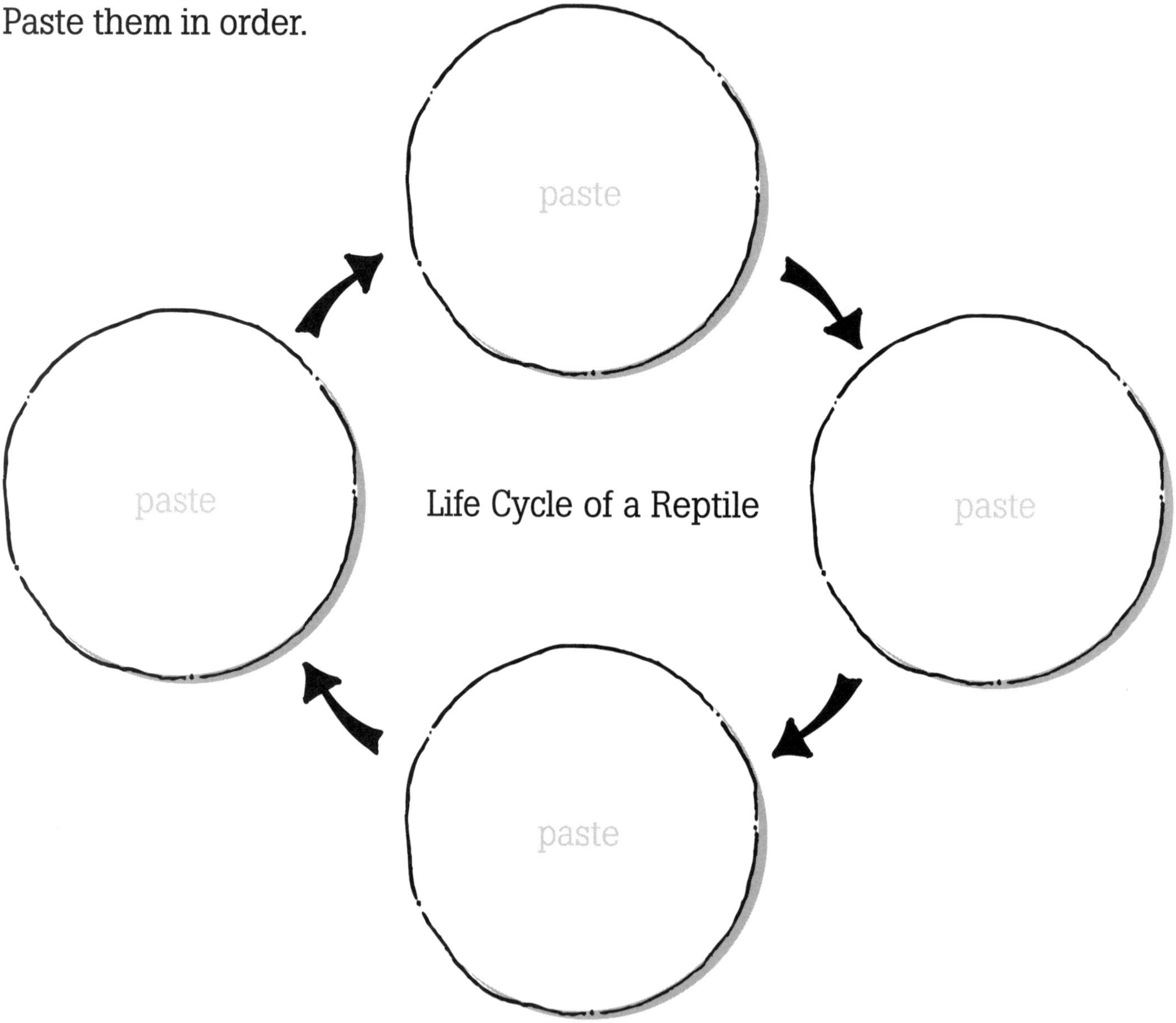

paste
paste
Life Cycle of a Reptile
paste
paste

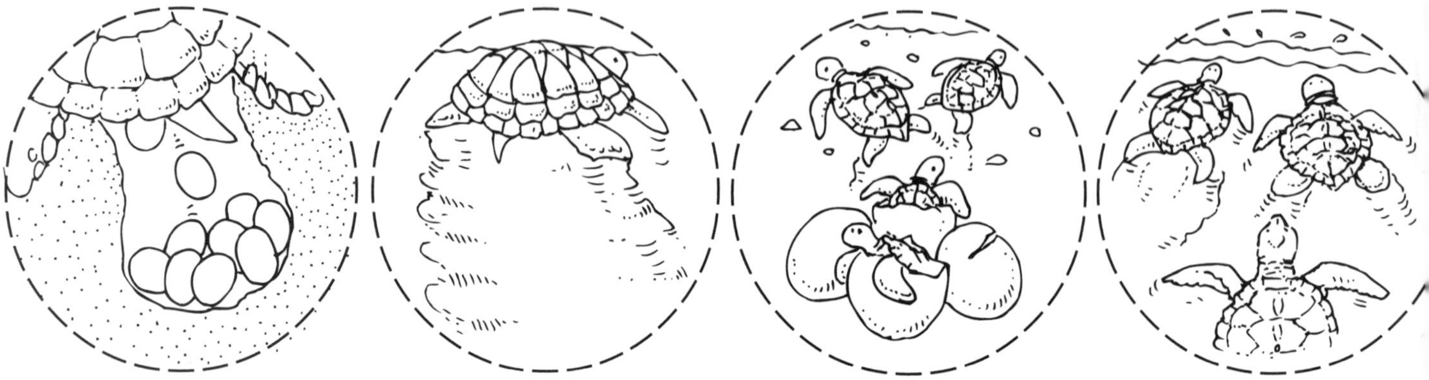

Animals Change and Grow

_____
Name

All animals are born, grow up, reproduce, and die. This is a life cycle.

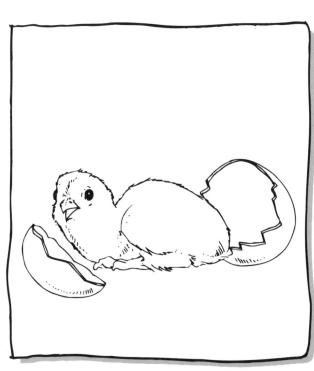

Some animals hatch from eggs.

Some animals are born alive.

1

Some babies look like their parents when they are born.

Some babies are a little different. They will soon look like their parents.

2

Some babies are very different. They will change a lot as they grow up. This big change is called metamorphosis (met-uh-mor-fah-sis).

- -

Some babies are helpless when they are born. These babies need a lot of care from their mothers.

Some babies are not helpless, but they still need their parents to protect and teach them.

Some babies don't need any care.

3

A salamander is an
amphibian. It changes
as it grows.

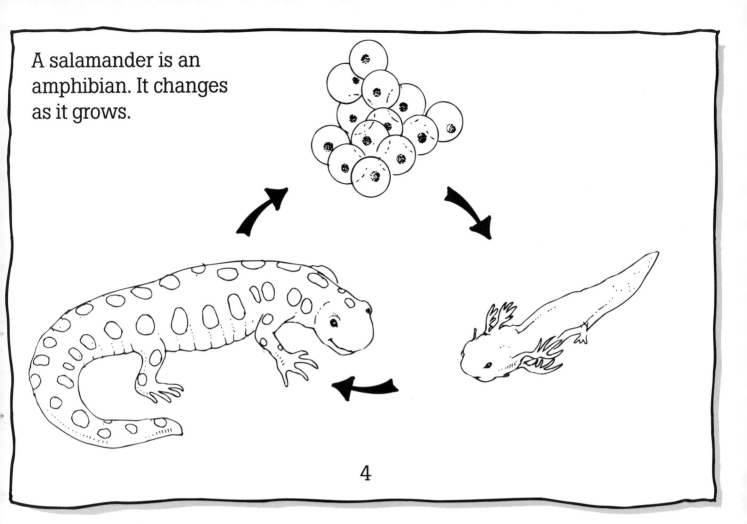

4

A parrot is a bird.
It changes as it grows.

5

A crocodile is a reptile.
It changes as it grows.

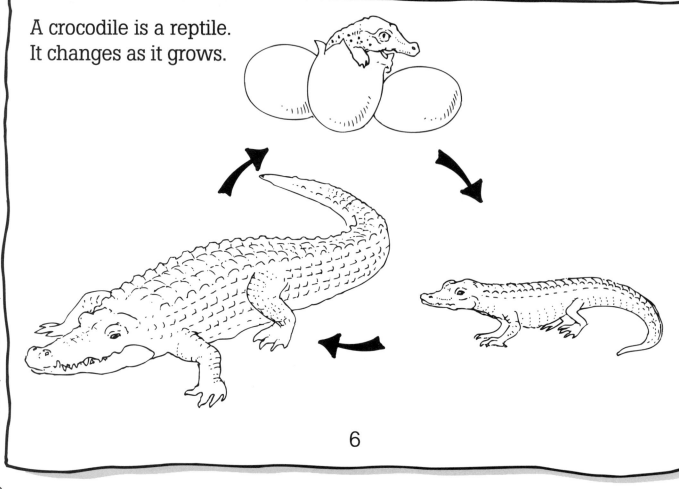

6

A swellshark is a fish.
It changes as it grows.

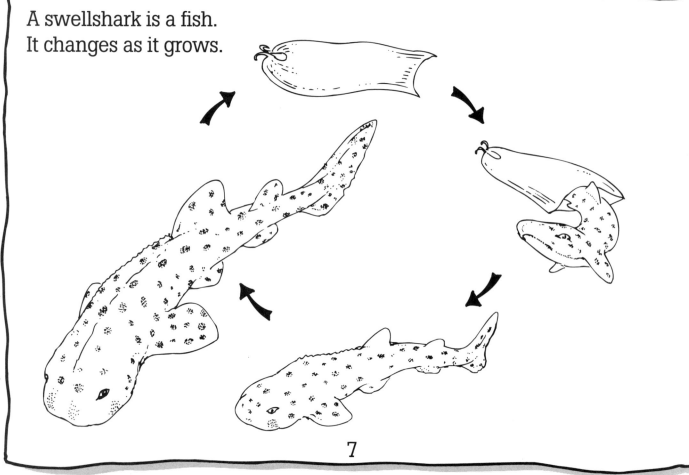

7

A kangaroo is a special
mammal. The mother has a
pouch. She raises her baby in
the pouch.

8

A duckbill platypus is a special
mammal, too. The mother lays eggs.
When the babies hatch from the eggs,
she feeds them milk from her body.

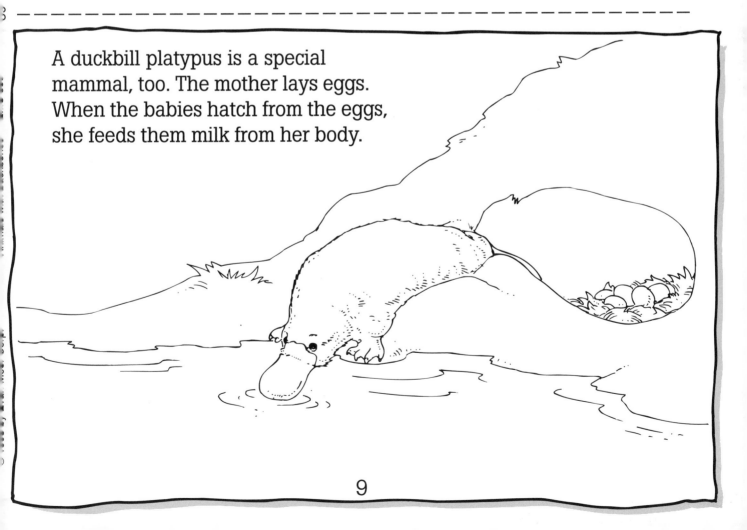

9

Vertebrates have developed different ways of acquiring food.

Finding Food

• Prepare a treat for the class. Something with a strong aroma works best— freshly popped corn, freshly baked cookies, or pizza. Hide it out of sight but in a place students can reach. Before students enter the classroom explain that there is a treat hidden somewhere in the room, and it is up to them to find it.

After the treat has been found, discuss what they did to find it. *(I smelled it and went to where I thought the smell was coming from. I looked around until I saw it. I heard Mark opening something, so I went to see if he had found the treat.)* Ask students to name the body parts they used to find the treat *(nose, eyes, ears)*.

My cat comes running when she hears the can opener. She thinks someone is opening a can of cat food.

Ask students to share ways they have seen animals use their senses to locate food.

• Reproduce the "How Animals Find Food" minibook on pages 43–47 for each student. Read pages 1–3 together and discuss how wild animals use their senses to locate food.

• Remind students that once animals locate their food they must get it. Brainstorm to list ways that animals do this.

> *Monkeys climb trees to get fruit.*
> *Cows and other grazers bite off grass.*
> *Lions chase zebras and kill them.*
> *Cats catch mice.*
> *Birds get worms out of the ground.*
> *Hawks grab little animals with their claws.*

Animals with Backbones • EMC 854

- Watch videos of animals as they gather or catch food. Add to the chart previously started.

- Write a page entitled "How Animals Find Food" for the class logbook.

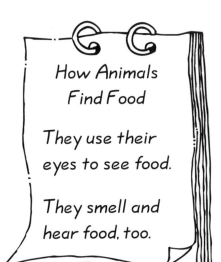

Plant Eaters

- Make an overhead transparency of page 48 showing plant eaters getting food. Use the pictures to help students identify physical adaptations that assist animals in collecting and eating food. Show one picture at a time and ask questions such as, "What is the giraffe eating? What helps the giraffe get the tree leaves?" Continue questioning with each picture.

- Read and discuss pages 4 and 5 of the "How Animals Find Food" minibook together. Have students complete the pages. (You may want to introduce the term "herbivore" at this time.)

- Write a page entitled "Plant Eaters" for the class logbook. Reproduce copies of the logbook form on page 4 for students to complete for their individual logbooks.

Plant Eaters

Apes use hands to pick plants to eat.

Cows and goats use teeth to chomp on grass.

Some birds use beaks to eat seeds and nuts.

Giraffes use long tongues to pick leaves.

Elephants use trunks to pick up plants.

Meat Eaters

- Make an overhead transparency of page 49 showing meat eaters getting food. Use the pictures to help students identify physical adaptations that assist animals in collecting and eating food. Show one picture at a time and ask questions such as, "What is the lion eating? What helped the lion catch its dinner? What is the lion using to eat the meat?" Continue questioning with each picture.

- Read and discuss minibook pages 6–9 together. Have students complete the pages. (You may want to introduce the term "carnivore" at this time.)

- Write a page entitled "Meat Eaters" for the class logbook. Reproduce copies of the logbook form on page 4 for students to complete for their individual logbooks.

- Reproduce page 50 for each student. They are to color the plant eaters and cross out the nonplant eaters.

- Reproduce page 51 for each student. They are to match the animal to its meal.

Meat Eaters

Lions and wolves run after prey.

Eagles and hawks dive down and grab prey.

Meat eaters use sharp claws to hold prey. They use sharp teeth to pull meat apart.

Extension Activity

If you keep classroom animals, conduct the following activity.

- Explain that even though they don't have to hunt for food, the animals in class have ways of knowing when food is put out for them. Have one student at a time feed the class animals and observe what each animal does. Ask questions such as:

    "What did the fish do when we dropped food into its bowl? How did the fish know the food was there?" (It saw the food. It felt the water move when the food was dropped in.)
    "How did the fish eat the food?" (It sucked it into its mouth.)
    "The hamster was in its cage when we gave it food. How did it know the food was there?" (It heard us. It smelled the food.)
    "How did the hamster eat the food?" (It picked it up with its paws and bit it with its teeth.)

- Reproduce copies of the logbook form on page 5 so the students can record what they did, what they saw, and what they learned about how animals know there is food to eat.

Animals with Backbones • EMC 854

How Animals Find Food

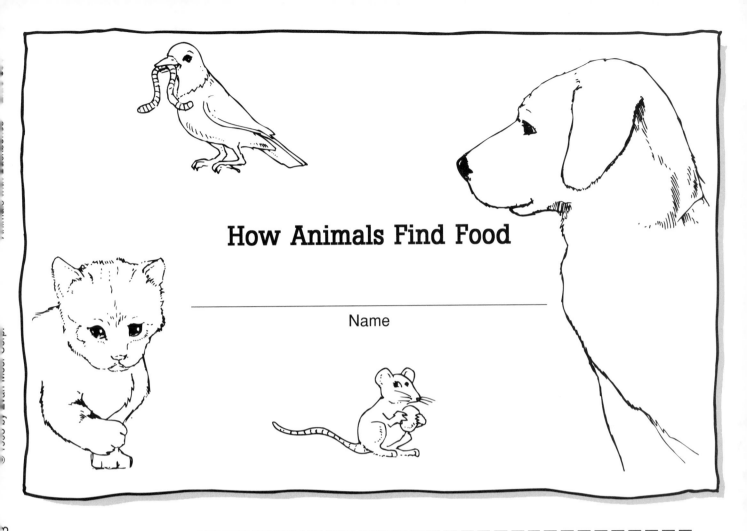

_____

Name

Animals use their senses to find food.

Some have such good eyesight they can see food far away. Birds of prey like eagles and hawks can see their prey from high in the sky.

1

Some animals can smell their food from far away.
Wolves can smell prey that is more than a mile away.

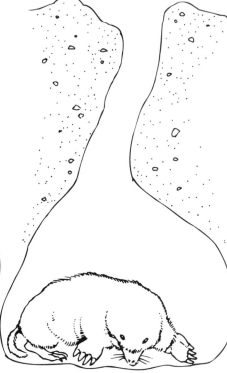

Moles smell food as they tunnel underground.
Draw a worm for this hungry mole.

2

A hunter can often hear prey before it can be seen.

The owl hears the mouse before he sees it.

3

When an animal finds it food, it must gather it up to eat.
Plant eaters do this in different ways.

teeth for pulling or biting off grass

a beak for sipping nectar

Some plant eaters have special parts to help them get their food.

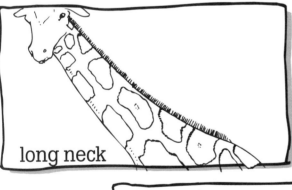

long neck

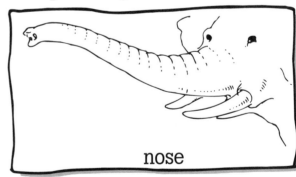

nose

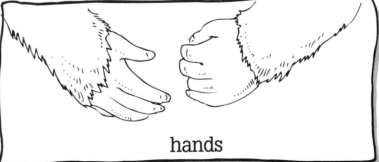

hands

Meat eaters must catch their dinners.

Small meat eaters, such as frogs and anteaters, use their tongues to capture food.

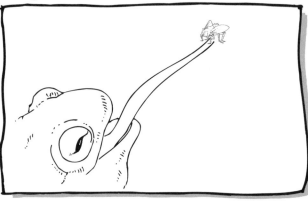 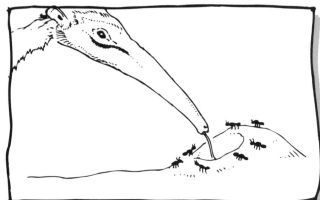

Circle the food a frog catches with its tongue.

 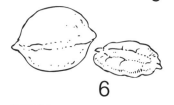

6

Large animals such as lions use speed to catch prey and sharp teeth and claws to kill it.

7

There are animals that use tricks to capture food.
A frogfish has a built-in bait to trick other fish. A smaller fish comes close to get the bait and the frogfish eats the fish.

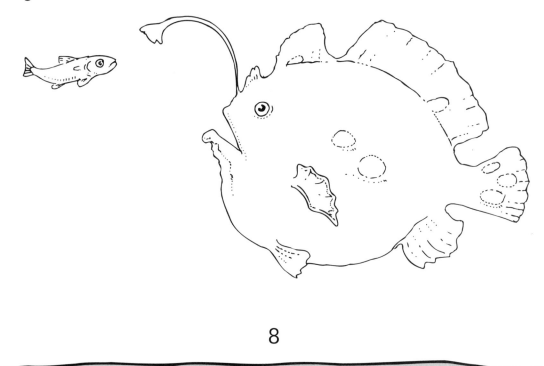

8

Some animals even use tools to get their dinner.

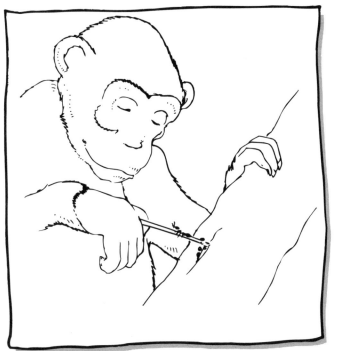 

Color the tools the animals are using.

9

Plant Eaters

Animals with Backbones • EMC 854

Meat Eaters

Animals with Backbones • EMC 854

Name _____

Plant Eaters

Color the plant eaters.
Mark an **X** on animals that don't eat plants.

50 Animals with Backbones • EMC 854

Name _____

Find My Dinner

Write the name of the animal that would eat this prey.

Word Box

frogfish	frog	wolf
eagle	mole	anteater
sea otter	lion	cat

Animals with Backbones • EMC 854

Vertebrate movements are adapted to the animal's needs.

How Animals Move

Build Movement Vocabulary

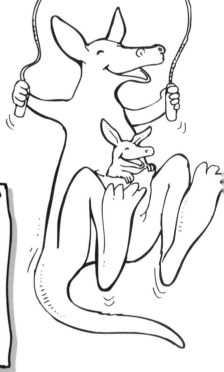

- Brainstorm to create a list of words that name ways animals move. Write these on a chart. Then list animals that move in each of the ways listed.

Ask questions to help students come up with more words. ("How does a snake move?") Introduce new words to increase student vocabulary. ("A snake slithers. A bear lumbers. A turtle creeps.") Add these to the list.

> fly — robin, bat, eagle   swim — fish, dog, whale
> run — wolf, cheetah   waddle — penguin, duck
> walk — deer, bird, pig   glide — flying squirrel, ray
> hop — kangaroo, frog, bird   slither — snake
> crawl — turtle, snake   trot — horse
> creep — turtle, sloth

Ask students to name the body parts used for different types of movements. Ask, "What does an animal use to swim? What is used to climb?" etc.

- Categorize the types of movements into those used by animals in different habitats. Make a chart entitled "Animal Movements" and divide and label it as shown. Have students list all the different ways animals in each habitat move.

- Provide nature magazines and trade books about vertebrates. Have students find pictures showing animals moving in the ways described on the list. Make additions and corrections to the "Animal Movements" chart.

Animal Movements	
on land run waddle walk trot climb hop slither	**in water** swim float dive
in the air fly dive glide	**underground** dig crawl

Animal Charades

You will need an open space for this activity. Have students mimic the various movements of animals as you name them—run, hop, crawl, waddle, fly, etc.

Then have everyone sit in a large circle. Call on one student. Have the student pick a card showing a picture of an animal. (Reproduce appropriate pictures from this unit. Paste each picture to a file card.) The student is to act out the movements of the animal as classmates try to identify it. Select a new student for each card.

Gather More Information

• Observe the class animals as they move. Name the types of movements they make and identify the body part(s) they use to make the movements.

  If you don't have classroom animals, bring in a goldfish and a friendly dog to observe for the lesson.

• View appropriate videos of vertebrates in motion, or read *Animals in Action—Child's First Library of Learning* (Time Life, 1989). Discuss what students learned from the videos. Ask questions about body adaptations for movement, such as:

  "What do animals that usually walk need?" *(paws, hooves, feet)*
  "What is needed if an animal usually swims?" *(webbed feet, flippers, fins, flukes)*
  "What do animals that climb need?" *(hands and feet, claws, tail that clings to things)*
  "What if an animal usually flies?" *(wings)*
  "What does an animal need if it digs tunnels?" *(sharp claws)*

Summary Activities

• Compare the movements of two of the animals observed, using a Venn diagram drawn on a sheet of butcher paper. For example:

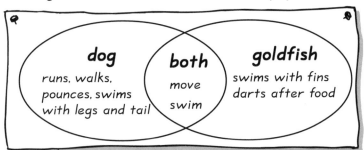

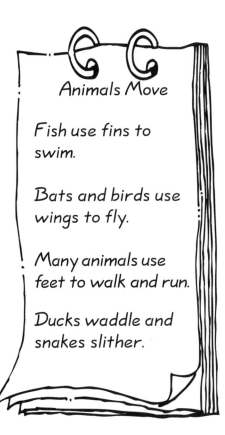

Animals Move

Fish use fins to swim.

Bats and birds use wings to fly.

Many animals use feet to walk and run.

Ducks waddle and snakes slither.

• Write a page entitled "Animals Move" for the class logbook. Reproduce copies of the logbook form on page 4 for individual logbooks.

• Reproduce page 55 for each student. They are to write ways the different animals shown might move.

• Reproduce the minibook on pages 56–58 for each student. Read and review the information together.

Make corrections and additions to the class logbook.

Extension Activity

Animal Footprints

• Look for footprints in the sandbox or dirt around the school or neighborhood. (Or make footprints in a damp box of sand with the feet of your classroom pets.)

Ask students to try to identify the prints (*bird, dog, etc.*). Have students assist in making castings of the prints, following these directions.

Materials

- footprints in sand or soil
- plaster of Paris
- milk carton
- stirring stick
- water
- tagboard strips 2" (5 cm) high (cut from an old file folder)
- stapler
- paintbrush

Steps to Follow

1. Mix the plaster of Paris in the milk carton, following the directions on the box.
2. Staple a strip of tagboard together to make a ring. Place it around the footprint.
3. Pour in a layer of plaster. Let it dry.
4. Carefully lift up the cast. Brush off the sand or dirt with a stiff paintbrush.

Have students look at each print and decide what type of foot made it (*bird claw, dog paw, duck foot, cat paw, etc.*).

Name _____

How Do I Move?

Write two ways in which each animal moves.

Feet, Fins, and Wings

_____
Name

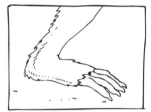  

How do animals get from place to place?
Let's read about some of the ways.

- -

Feet, paws, and hooves are used to walk and run.

monkey

bear

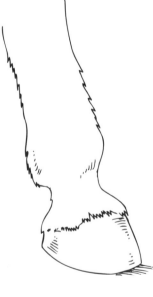
horse

Circle the feet that can also trot.

1

Hands, feet, tails, beaks, and claws help animals climb around.

Circle the parts of each animal that are being used to climb.

2

Fins and flukes help water animals swim.

Some land animals can swim, too.

3

This animal slithers.

4

Wings carry birds up into the sky.

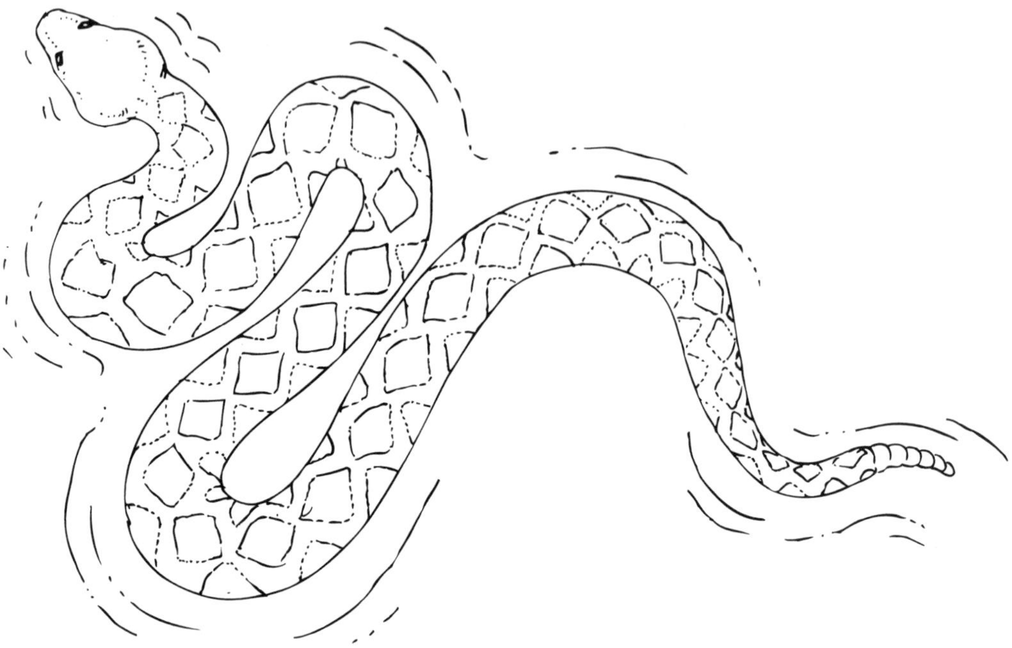

Draw the mammal that flies.

5

Vertebrates have developed many forms of self-defense.

Animal Defenses

- Begin a discussion of the ways animals in the wild protect themselves by asking students to recall what their pets do when they are frightened. *(My dog barks and snarls. My cat runs and hides under the bed. Sometimes my cat uses its claws to scratch. My canary makes a lot of noise and flaps her wings. My lizard sits very still on its rock. Sometimes it runs under the rock.)*

- If you have classroom pets, continue the discussion by having students observe what the animals in the classroom do when they are frightened. *(The hamster runs into its sleeping box. The fish hide in the plants. The lizard goes under its rock. The parakeet makes a lot of noise.)*

- Brainstorm ways wild animals protect themselves. Record these on a page entitled "Animal Defenses" for the class logbook.

- Read books such as *How to Hide a Parakeet and Other Birds* by Ruth Heller (Putnam Publishing Group, 1995); *How to Hide a Polar Bear and Other Mammals* by Ruth Heller (Putnam Publishing Group, 1994); *Eyewitness Junior Books Amazing Animal Disguises* by Sandie Sowler (Alfred A. Knopf, 1982); *Amazing Armored Animals* by Sandie Sowler (Alfred A. Knopf, 1992). Ask students to recall what they learned from the readings. Teach the terms "protective coloration" and " camouflage" at this time.

- Add new information to the class logbook and make any corrections. Reproduce the logbook form on page 4 for students to write about animal defenses for their individual logbooks.

Animal Defenses

Some use teeth and claws.

Some run away.

Some hide.

Skunks make a bad smell.

Birds peck.

A turtle goes into its shell.

A snake bites. It can poison you.

Protective Coloration

- Explore protective coloration using colored construction paper and small realistic models of animals. (Or use colored photographs cut from nature magazines.)

Hide some of the animal models around the classroom by placing them against appropriately colored backgrounds. Place others against contrasting colors. Have students try to find all of the animal models.

When all the animals have been located, ask students to explain which were the easiest and which were the hardest to find and why. Have students use sheets of construction paper and the animal models to show how protective coloration works.

Ask students to explain how it is helpful for an animal to change color if it lives in a place that is covered in snow and ice all winter.

- Reproduce the logbook form on page 5 for each student to use to record what they did, what they saw, and what they learned.

- Reproduce page 61 for each student. They are to locate the animals hiding in the picture.

Summary Activities

- Reproduce pages 62–68 for each student. Cut and staple pages 62–67 together to make a riddle book. Students will cut out the pictures on page 68 and paste them in the book to answer the riddles.

- Reproduce page 69 for each student. They are to write what each animal uses for self-defense.

"If I put the green frog on green paper it is hard to see. If I put it on white paper it is easy to see."

Who Am I?
An Animal Defenses Riddle Book

Name

Animals with Backbones • EMC 854

Name _____

Find the Animals

Color the animals hiding here.

Animals with Backbones • EMC 854

Who Am I?

An Animal Defenses Riddle Book

_____

Name

- -

If I stamp my feet, look out!
I'm getting ready to spray a bad smell.

paste

1

If danger comes my way, I pull my head and feet inside my shell.

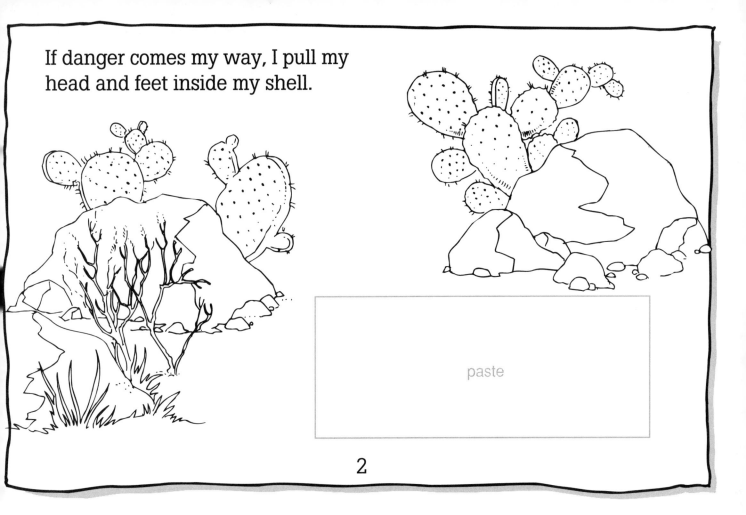

paste

2

If you hear my rattle, go away.
If you stay, I might bite you.

paste

3

When I hear danger, I fall
over and pretend to be dead.

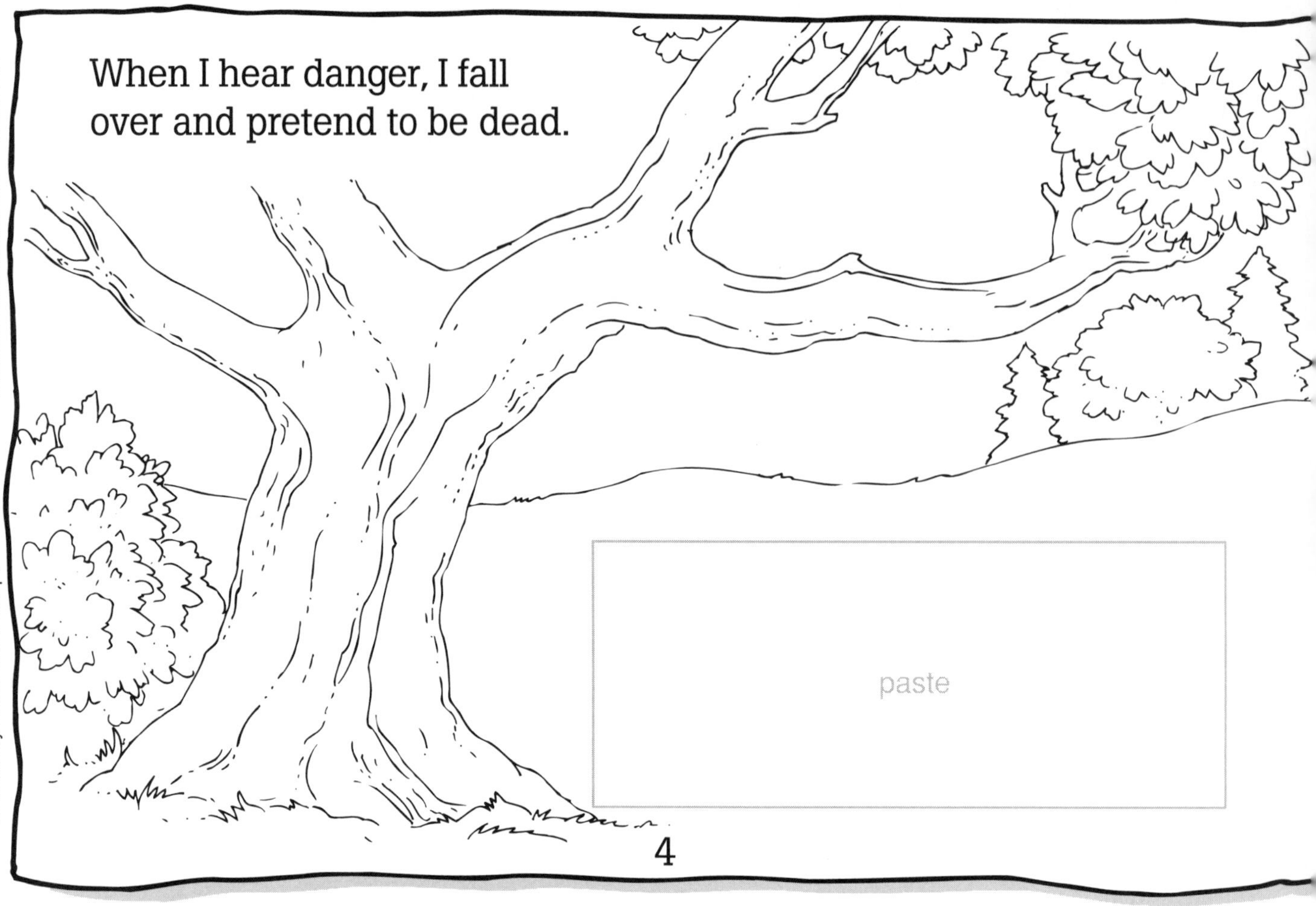

paste

4

Nobody can see me when I
hang on to a piece of sea grass.

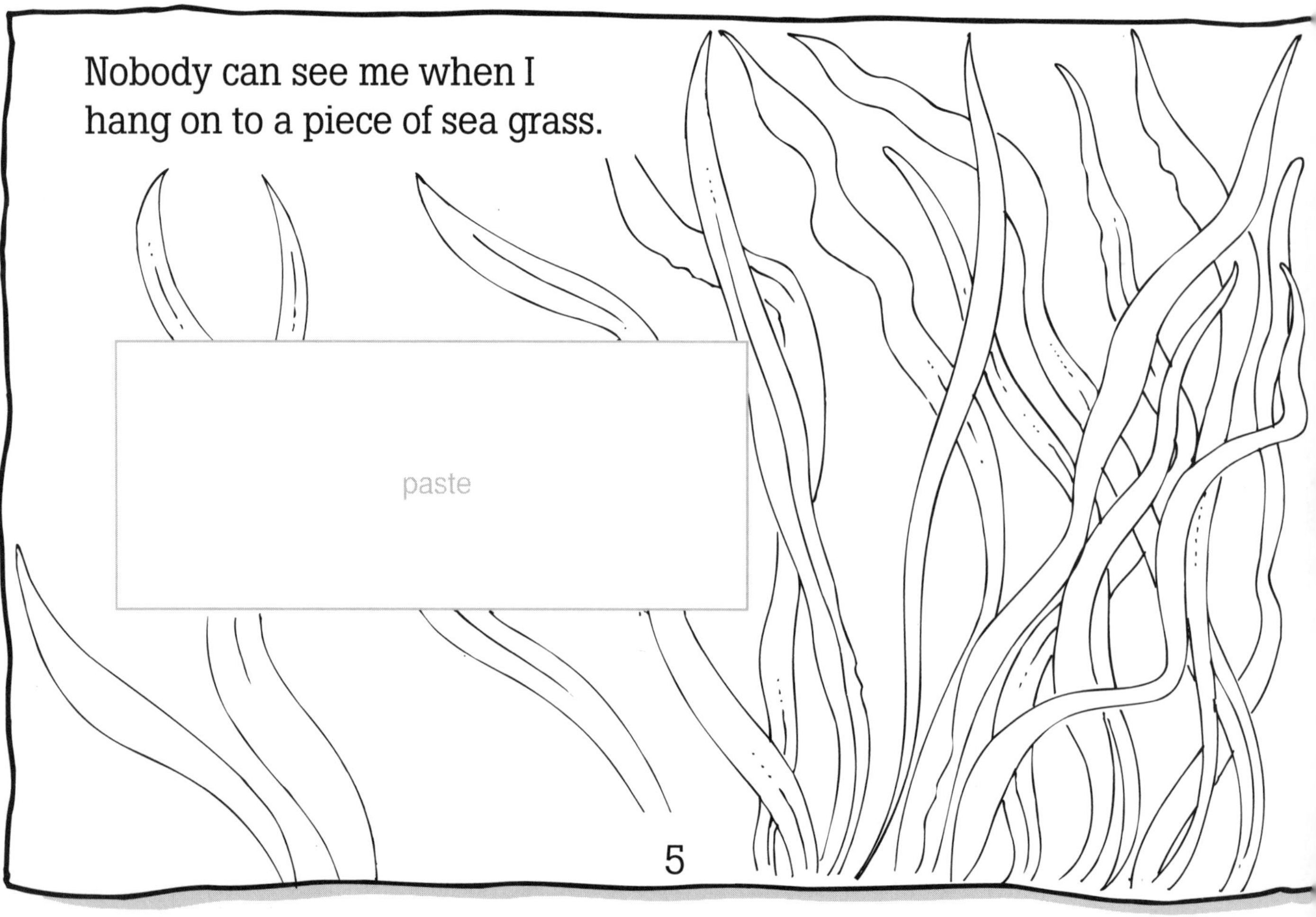

paste

5

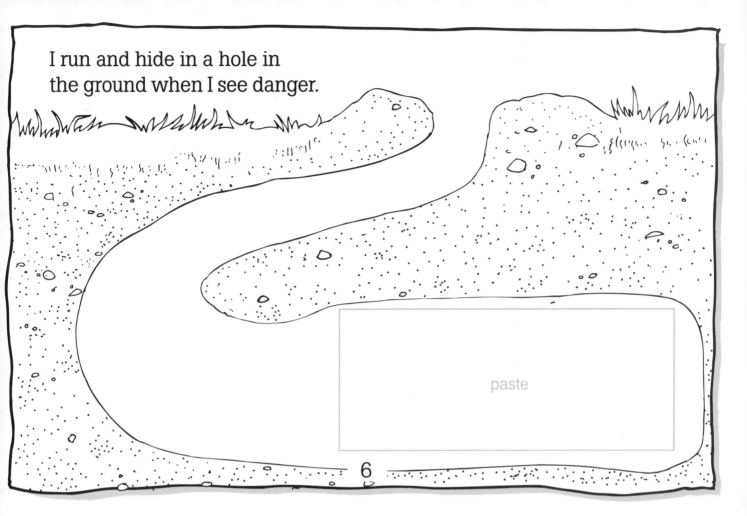

I run and hide in a hole in
the ground when I see danger.

paste

6

I'm colorful and cute. But don't touch me. I'll poison you.

paste

7

When I hear danger, I curl myself up.
If you touch me, my needlelike spines will stick in your skin.

paste

8

Don't mess with me. I have sharp teeth and claws.
I scratch and bite.

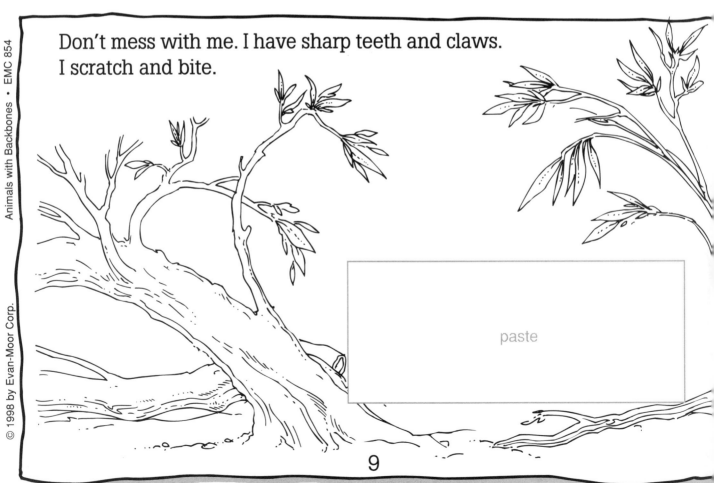

paste

9

In winter my feathers turn white. I sit still in the snow to hide from danger.

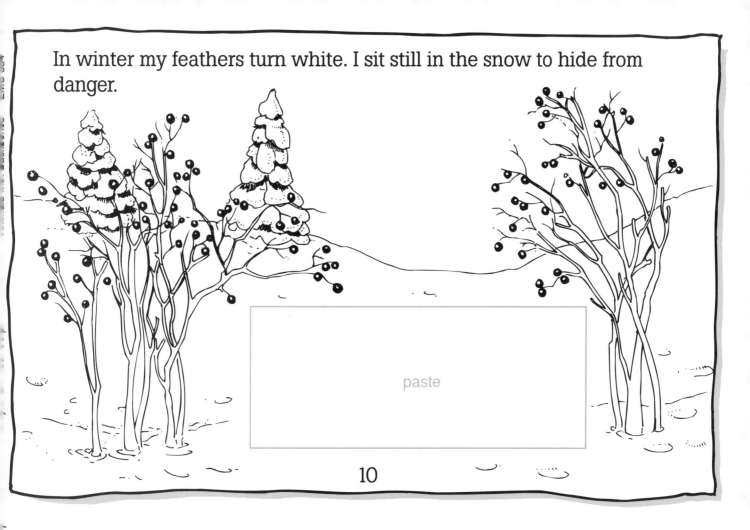

paste

10

I lay on the bottom of the ocean.
I am covered in sand.
Only my eyes show I am here.

paste

11

Cut out the pictures.
Paste them in your animal riddle book.

Name _____

What I Use for Protection

Write the name of an animal that uses each kind of protection.

1. A _____ uses poison.

2. A _____ uses claws and teeth.

3. A _____ uses its shape and color.

4. An _____ plays dead.

5. A _____ runs and hides.

6. A _____ uses a bad smell.

7. A _____ has a hard shell.

8. A _____ has sharp spines.

porcupine	skunk	opossum
leopard	rabbit	rattlesnake
pipefish	turtle	

69   Animals with Backbones • EMC 854

Some vertebrates build homes.

What Is a Home?

- Encourage students to give reasons why they live in homes. Write their ideas on the chalkboard.

- Have students describe their pets' homes. Ask, "Do your pets have special homes? What are they called?" *(We have a dog house for our big dog. My brother keeps his pet snake in a terrarium. My parakeet lives in a big cage. My cat lives in the house with us, but she has a special bed.)* Ask, "Why are homes important for pets?" *(They need a place to be safe from danger. They need food and a place to sleep. They would get lost if they didn't have a home.)*

> *A home is where we eat.*
>
> *We need a place to sleep.*
>
> *A home keeps us safe.*
>
> *It's where our family can be together.*

If you have classroom animals, observe and discuss their homes.

- Reproduce page 73 for each student. They are to draw their pet and explain why it needs a special home. Students who do not have a pet can draw and write about a pet they would like to have.

Wild Animals' Homes

- Discuss whether wild animals need homes. Guide students with questioning to reach these conclusions:

  Most wild animals don't have homes.
  Some wild animals build homes.
  Animals build homes to have a safe place to raise a family.

- Write a page entitled "Animal Homes" for the class logbook. Reproduce the logbook form on page 4 for students to write about animal homes for their individual logbooks.

> *Animals Homes*
>
> *Some animals build homes.*
>
> *They want a place that is dry and warm.*
>
> *They want a place that is safe.*
>
> *They want a place to raise babies.*

Animal Builders

- View videos of animal builders in action and read books such as *Animals That Build Homes* by Kyle Carter (Rourke Book Company, 1995) or *Books for Young Explorers, Animals That Build Their Homes* by Robert McClung (National Geographic Society, 1976). Have students share what they learned from the reading. Make additions or corrections to the class logbook.

- If you live in an area where it is possible, take students on a walk to look for homes built by animals. Point out examples as you walk along. Ask, "What kind of home is it? What animal might have built it? What is it made of?" (Prepare your route ahead of time by taking a look at the neighborhood, a nearby park, or a vacant lot for homes. Look for birds' nests, gopher holes, squirrels' nests, mole runs, holes in trees where animals live, etc.)

When you return to school, have students illustrate and write about one or more homes they saw.

Animals' Homes Minibook

- Reproduce pages 74–78 for each student. Read the pages together to review facts about animal builders.

- Reproduce page 79 for each student. Have them read and follow the directions to locate each animal's home.

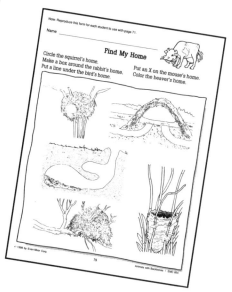

Make a Report

Each student is to paint a picture of an animal builder and its home. Then the students will write a paragraph describing the home and explaining why the animal needs a home.

Provide time for students to share their pictures and paragraphs with the class or display the reports on a bulletin board.

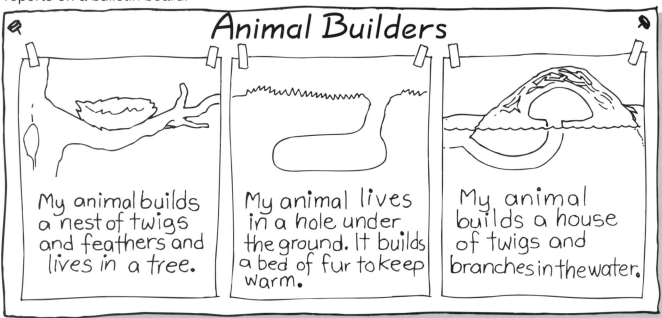

Check for Understanding

To assess student understanding of the reasons for animal homes, have students build a home for an imaginary animal.

Materials

- an assortment of building materials such as:
    straw, twigs, leaves
    small pieces of wood
    small cardboard containers
    raffia, yarn, string
    scraps of paper
- imaginary animal cards on page 80
- scissors
- glue

Steps to Follow

1. Divide the class into small groups.
2. Give each group an imaginary animal card. They are to read the description and decide what kind of home the animal might make.
3. Using available materials, each group will construct a small "home" for their animal.
4. When the homes are complete, have one student present their group's construction to the class, explaining the reasons for building such a home.

72

Note: Reproduce this form for each student to use with page 70.

Name ______________________________

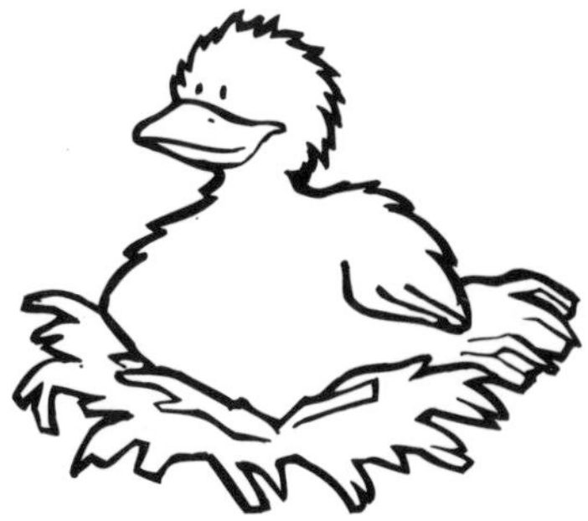

My Pet's Home

Draw your pet and its home.

Write to tell why your pet needs a special home.

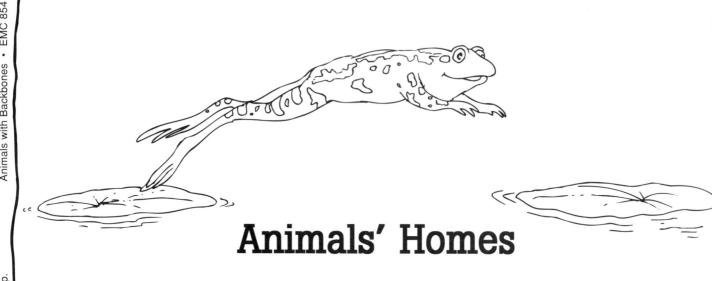

Animals' Homes

_____
Name

Most wild animals don't have homes. They don't need a special place to stay. They go around looking for food. They sleep wherever they are. They have their babies wherever they are.

74

Some animals build homes. They build homes to be safe. They build homes to raise their babies.

1

These birds build nests for their babies.

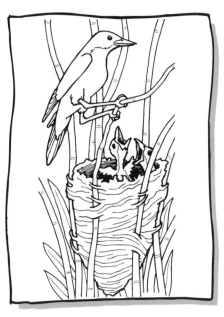

A robin builds a nest of twigs and mud.

A reed warbler weaves a nest of grass.

A flamingo builds a nest of mud.

2

This fish's nest is in the sand.

3

The mouse's nest is made of grass stems.

4

A beaver builds a lodge of tree branches.

5

Some animals build underground homes.

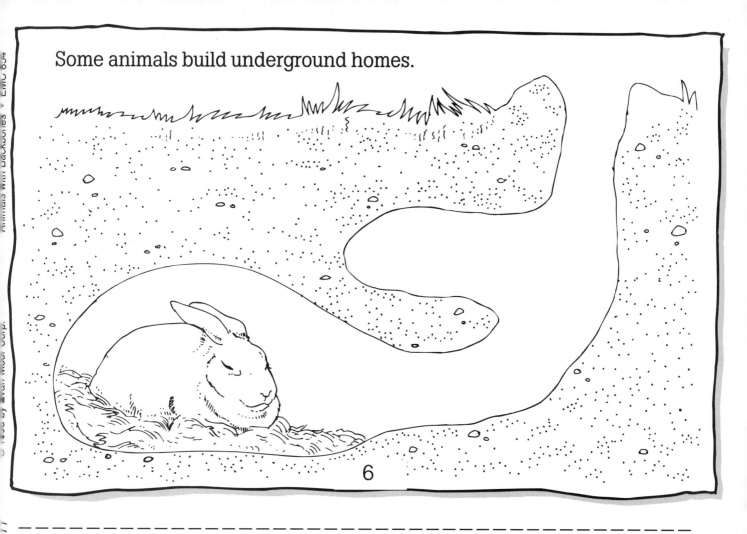

6

An alligator builds a nest of plants and mud.

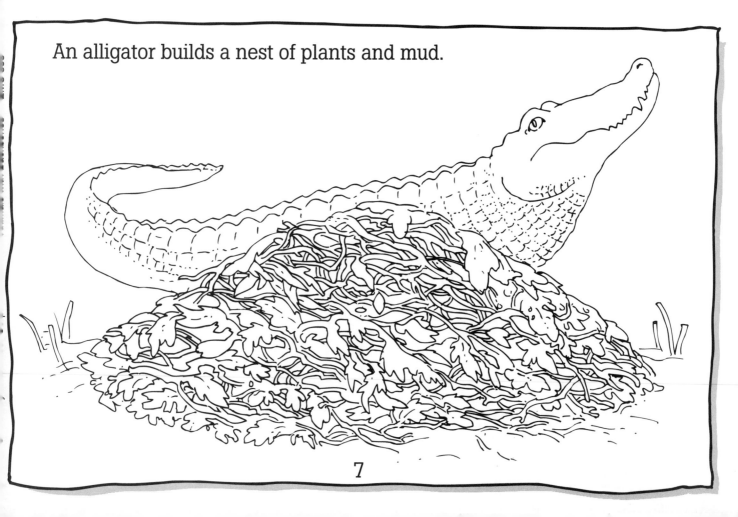

7

Some animals live together in groups. Prairie dogs dig underground tunnels and rooms.

8

Some animals borrow homes. The elf owl lives in a hole made by a woodpecker.

Some animals carry their homes.

9

Name _____

Find My Home

Circle the squirrel's home.
Make a box around the rabbit's home.
Put a line under the bird's home.

Mark an **X** on the mouse's home.
Color the beaver's home.

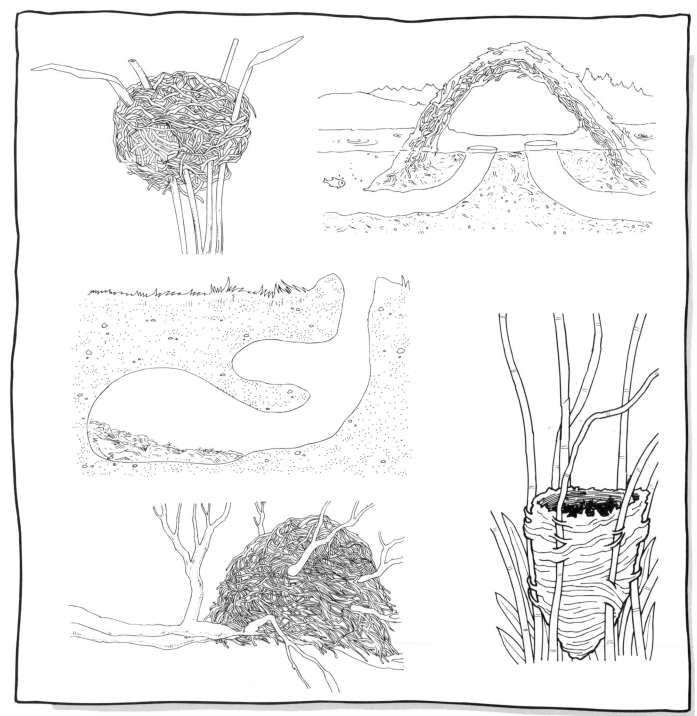

I am a small scaly animal.
I have six legs with sharp claws.
I look for food at night.

I am a small flying animal.
I have two tiny babies at a time.
I like to hide in bushes.

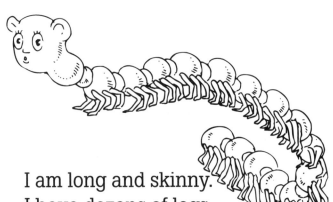

I am long and skinny.
I have dozens of legs.
I can climb anything.
I like to be covered in soft leaves
when I sleep.

I am round and covered in spines.
I move very slowly on my short legs.
It is hard for me to climb up or down.

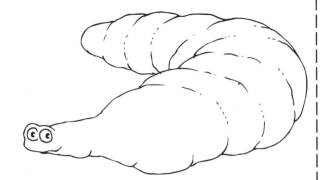

I am big and soft.
I can crawl into little openings.
I like to live with a group, but I
want my own room.

I am big and covered in green fur.
I curl up in a huge ball when I sleep.
I need a home that helps me hide.

Animals with Backbones • EMC 854